Walks from Your Car

C000091983

Upper
Wharfedale

by
Colin Speakman

Dalesman Books
1989

The Dalesman Publishing Company Ltd.,
Clapham, Lancaster, LA2 8EB

First published 1989

© Colin Speakman 1989

ISBN: 0 85206 965 0

Printed by Swannack Brown & Co., Ltd., Hull, England

Contents

Cover map by Barbara Yates
Maps in text by David W. Holdsworth A.S.T.D

Upper Wharfedale

IF opinions remain eternally divided about which is the most beautiful of the Yorkshire Dales, undoubtedly the most popular in the sense of most visited, is Wharfedale – largely because of its accessibility to a huge centre of population. But it is also an area of exceptional interest for the rambler, whether the experienced fellsman or the Sunday afternoon stroller. It varies from a rich, rolling lowland landscape in its lower sections below Wetherby, to largely underrated but often exceptionally beautiful central sections between Ilkley, Otley and Harewood among the specially protected landscapes of the Yorkshire Dales National Park – Upper Wharfedale.

Because of its popularity this is an area which hardly lacks guide books. Indeed over the last twenty years the growth of books, leaflets and maps about the dale has been truly phenomenal, reflecting a national explosion of interest in walking and the countryside which none but the most short-sighted and narrow-minded can regret.

So why then yet another book of walks about this particular ramblers' paradise?

Quite simply this is a book for those many people who do not have time or energy for a full day's walk in Upper Wharfedale, who perhaps are on holiday, visiting the area or with young children (all these are excellent family walks which can be managed by any healthy and energetic five year old – or younger in a parent's papoose). This is also a book for those people who are simply not quite as young as they used to be, or aren't really used to leaving their car to discover what a remarkable and beautiful footpath heritage awaits them in Wharfedale.

No apology then if this is a book of "Walks for Softies" – mainly easy or very easy walks that can be done by an average person in an afternoon. All of us at certain times in our lives – or at certain times of the year, for example on winter afternoons – need short walks which can give a real feel and flavour of the countryside without requiring too much time and energy.

So this book contains ten walks, none of which are more than five miles in length, none of which are strenuous, all of which can be done to and from a parked car or, with a little careful planning, by local bus services either from Skipton or Ilkley.

But they are all really country walks. You will need warm outdoor clothing and waterproofs at all times of the year except for a relatively few days in high summer when soaring temperatures and clear skies allow a little latitude – but a safe rule even then is to have at least a waterproof with you. Heavy shoes or even trainers will be adequate for many of the walks, but others have rough or muddy sections of footpath where boots with their extra protection are strongly advised – albeit of the modern lightweight variety.

Most paths will be easy to find but there are places where pathfinding needs a little care. In the Yorkshire Dales paths across fields or pasture are largely indicated by stiles in drystones walls which vary from the traditional stone "squeezer" or step stiles to the modern wooden National Park ladder stiles – all of which you have to be fairly agile to cross, with care needed particularly in wet weather where surfaces are wet. But they often go through field gates – and the rule is if you find it closed or it isn't clearly propped open, close it behind you. And only the most heavily used paths are visible on the ground. Most rights-of-way as their name implies are a right of passage across private land, so please keep to the line of the path wherever possible.

Paths, in the National Park areas at least, are usually well signed where they leave the road, and many but not all routes are waymarked along the way with the standard yellow arrow or markers for public footpaths and blue for public bridleways.

All routes in this book have been well tried and tested over many years and are free from obstruction – at the time of writing at least.

Maps in the text are for guidance and in most cases will prove adequate, but we have indicated the appropriate 1:25:000 Outdoor Leisure or Pathfinder Maps for each walk which offer far greater accuracy and detail than any written text or sketch map can provide. Highly recommended too are the special pocket maps for walkers drawn by Arthur Gemmell of Otley which cover most of these walks. These are available from local shops or by post from Stile Maps, Mercury House, Otley, West Yorkshire LS21 3HE.

Whenever you walk in the Dales, whether within or outside the National Park, please respect the life and work of the countryside. Keep dogs under control, particularily during the lambing season in March and April when the presence of a dog even on a lead can be a disruptive influence. Keep to paths across farmland and take litter home, and when walking across the long grass of meadowland, particularily in spring, please keep in single file to minimise erosion and damage. Such thoughtful behaviour will ensure a continuing welcome for walkers by the farming community in the Yorkshire Dales.

Calvary

A walk from Ilkley on the less well known side of the valley taking in some delightful woodland paths with some unusual Wharfedale views – and a remarkable religious shrine.

Distance: 4 miles.   Time required: 2-2½ hours.

Terrain: Woodland and riverside paths. Gentle climbs. Boots advised – some places can be extremely muddy after rain, when wellingtons are recommended, particularily through the woodland sections.

Parking: In the town's main car park behind Brook Street. It is usually possible to park by the river bridge.

Public Transport: Frequent MetroTrain services from Leeds and Bradford; bus West Yorkshire RCC bus services from Leeds, Bradford, Otley, Keighley, and Skipton.

Refreshment: Ilkley – choice of cafes and inns. Toilets by central car park and opposite railway station.

Maps: OS Pathfinder SE04/14 Keighley and Ilkley. The Ilkley Moor Footpath Map (West Riding Ramblers' Association).

THOUGH Ilkley is not quite Upper Wharfedale, it is the point when the true higher Dales countryside begins. It is also particularly rich in history having been in turn a Celtic settlement, a Roman Camp, an Anglian village and a 19th century moorland health spa. It also makes an excellent starting or finishing point for a ramble and as good introduction as any to the special delights of Wharfedale.

From car park, bus or rail station, make your way past Ilkley Church and the grassy remains of the Roman fort of Olicana alongside, towards the main bridge over the River Wharfe. Do not cross the bridge, but take the path reached down steps before the bridge to the riverside, walking upstream through the little riverside park and by the boating stage to Ilkley Old Bridge – a narrow hump-backed bridge picturesquely arching across the river shallows.

The earliest recorded bridge at Ilkley was in existence here in the 16th century. No doubt bridges existed on this important crossing point of the Wharfe since medieval times to replace the deep and

1 mile

dangerous ford served by Roman roads, which can still be seen some distance below the bridge and which the original Roman fort by the church was built to guard.

The present bridge dates from the later 17th century, and is a typical Dales hump-back construction, with powerful breakwater piers to split the force of river that can rise with quite alarming speed after winter storms. Once the only crossing point of the river between Otley and Bolton Abbey, it is now closed to motor traffic. The large metal bridge – Middleton Bridge – which now carries the town's main traffic over the river was only opened in the first years of the present century when the Middleton Estates were developed. The Old Bridge has another claim to fame, between Ilkley and Windermere (see the author's *Dales Way* in the Dalesman Long Distance Walks series).

Cross the old bridge, going sharp left at the far side of the bridge on to the riverside path. Follow the path upstream until it joins the Nesfield road at a crossroads. Cross over and take the road opposite but go first left along Owler Park Road. This is a suburban road past expensive houses with increasingly fine views across the dale to the high ridge of Ilkley Moor as you ascend.

Where the road turns right towards Owler Park Farm, at a handsome house, Austby, your way (signed) is over a stile, just to the left, leading deep into a wood. Follow the path as its snakes through the wood, leading over another stile into a field. Keep ahead to where the path descends to a wood to cross a stile, fords a shallow stream before climbing to another stile. It then goes over a footbridge, over a second stream and around to a third stile just to the left. There are magnificent views along the dale to Addingham High Moor and beyond from here.

Now cross the field keeping left towards the farm, Low Austby, and stile ahead. Do not cross this stile but turn right, uphill and alongside the fence, climbing up to a stile in the fence in the top corner, keeping ahead by two great old oaks to a field gate ahead. Be sure to close it behind you.

A green way, over which geese usually wander, bears to the right below a garden. Keep on until you reach a stile beyond a gate which joins the house drive. The right-of-way leads along the drive to a crossroads. Turn right along a metalled track to where the track bears right downhill and the way (also signed) goes through a field gate ahead. Take this track, alongside a hedge to the next field gate, which leads to a metalled drive with a stream and wood to the the left and a house to the right.

As you approach a dense area of woodland, you will notice a wooden entrance signed Calvary. This leads to a gateway with a Latin inscription though which is a narrow grove of 14 mounted relief sculptures – the Stations of the Cross, scenes from Christ's last hours as he suffered on his way to Calvary. The reliefs, carved from fine sandstone, were executed by a young Italian artist, guest of Mr Peter Middleton, owner of Middleton Lodge and the Middleton estates in the 1880s. The Middletons were a long established Yorkshire Catholic family and this grove and the stone grotto with its wooden crosses "The Calvary" were an expression of their ancient faith. Please treat the area with respect.

Return the way you have to come to the drive but instead of turning left look for another permissive path, this time through the rhododendrons of Middleton Lodge to a Roman altar which has been placed not far from the house and chapel – it is reputedly a Votive altar dedicated to the goddess Verbeia, Roman goddess of the Wharfe, and was placed here in the 17th century by Sir William Middleton.

Turn left at the altar to the grotto surrounded by a paved area ahead. A path to the left of the grotto leads to a gate into the lane.

The old Middleton Lodge has been a Catholic sanctuary and monastery for many years and paths through the grounds have been open to the public. Should cirmcumstances change, you should continue along the drive by Calvary (a public bridleway) and turn right in the lane past the cottages.

Otherwise keep straight ahead as the lane bends left to reach a crossroads some 120 metres ahead to a second crossroads, this time with the Beamsley Road. Go left here but then turn first right along Hardings Lane, signed Middleton Hospital. About 50 metres past a rather palatial house, The Hollies, a stile and sign leads to a path across a broad somewhat muddy field towards Middleton Woods ahead – again there are fine views as you descend, this time across the rooftops of Ilkley town to the Cow and Calf Rocks on Ilkley Moor.

At the stile into the woods, bear left along the path which gradually drops through the woods. These are magnificent woodlands, rich in beech and oak and heavily scented with bluebells in spring. Keep left at a junction down a shallow ravine, eventually reaching a footbridge over a narrow stream before the path bears right to follow a tongue of woodland between house gardens to a stile on Curly Hill. Don't worry too much if you take one of several branching paths by mistake – most rejoin at the same point.

Go left here for a short way, but then take the first path right, over another stile and down steps, crossing a footbridge and heading for the playing fields ahead. The path goes by the swimming pool and crosses the road. Keep ahead across the grass to the river, turning right to Ilkley Bridge, the comforts of the town, and car, bus or train home.

Haw Pike

This walk to a less well known summit offers exceptionally fine panoramic views of Wharfedale, without having to climb great heights.

Distance: 4½ miles   Time required: 2-2½ hours.

Parking: Because Addingham has no official public car park, park in Bark Lane on the Bolton Abbey road from Ilkley just beyond Addingham Church where there is a wide tarmac verge and safe parking on the roadside near to Addingham suspension bridge – the end of the walk.

Public Transport: Hourly buses from Leeds, and Skipton (service 784), Ilkley Railway Station (Services 784, 765) and from Keighley (765, 762). Alight at The Fleece and walk towards Skipton before turning right up Sugar Hill (lane by public conveniences) to join the walk by the old railway line.

Refreshment: The Fleece Inn on the main A65 at Addingham serves coffee, lunches and pub snacks during normal opening times. Other pubs and cafes in the village.

Maps: OS Pathfinder SE05/15 Bolton Abbey and Blubberhouses.

WALK along Bark Lane in the Bolton Abbey direction to the junction with the B6160 from Addingham village centre. Cross and turn left and almost immediately turn right into Springfield Road, a narrow lane by the backs of houses and gardens. At the end keep straight ahead by more gardens to continue down an alleyway leading to a stile and tiny pedestrian gate. Cross here into a field, but bear left across a farm track to a tall wooden gap stile in the fence on the left. This gives access to a narrow stony path which crosses to the old Ilkley-Bolton-Abbey railway line – an early and much lamented victim of the Beeching axe in 1965. Turn left alongside what remains of the old railway embankment to emerge by an old railway bridge where Sugar Hill, the lane from the centre of Addingham to be used for anyone coming by bus, joins the route.

Turn right here but take the first track again to the right, signposted by a cottage which soon passes a school. Just past a ruined barn a kissing gate, left, signed, indicates the line of the path which follows the edge

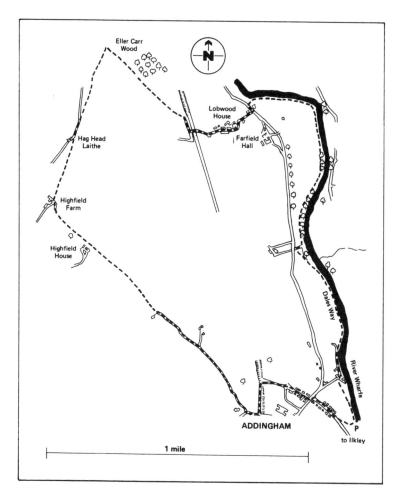

of the fields alongside the farm track.

This is a steady, but easy, climb rewarded by magnificent views of Beamsley Beacon to your right, the conical summit which in Tudor times was one of the great chain of beacons used to alert communities to major events or warn them of threats such as the Spanish Armada of 1588.

The path continues alongside the farmtrack which soon becomes an overgrown way. Eventually you are in a narrow field. Keep ahead, over two more stiles heading towards a fine Georgian farm, Highfield House, ahead. The next stile is over the fence ahead, immediately to the right and behind the farm. Keep ahead with a wire fence to your right to the next stile in the stone wall ahead, by the gate. The path now heads towards Highfield Farm, but before the farm bear right to a stile marked with white paint in the wall by the wall corner.

Your way is now in the same direction across a shallow dip in the pasture ahead to a steep step stile you will see in the wall directly ahead. The next stile, by a ruined barn, is murderously steep and should be only tackled by the most agile, the better part of valour being to bear left around the edge of the wall by the ruin. This low hill is Haw Pike, though the actual summit trig point is some distance to the left.

The way is now to the right along a green track through a gate, but in the next field bear right away from the track to the wall corner where there is another stone step stile – this time with a magnificent view of the dale, with Simons Seat, Bolton Bridge and Bolton Abbey itself as well as the whole sweep of the River Wharfe in a matchless setting spread out before you.

The path now descends to open pasture in the same direction towards a wood in the dip of the hill – Lob Wood – but after about 200 metres where the path is intersected by a path from the right (not visible on the ground), veer sharp right towards the wall corner. This emerges immediately above another little wood – Eller Carr Wood – below, where you'll see a steepish step stile just above the wall corner (which can be avoided by going to the field gate to the right).

Cross now to the bottom corner of the next field. Here the path goes through a gate and close to the old railway line once again to a second gate and a track, left, under the buttresses of an old railway bridge. This leads to Lobwood House Farm. Keep to the right of the large new cow house and along the farm drive to the main B6160 road.

Cross extremely carefully (there is no pavement and traffic travels fast) to turn left and face the oncoming traffic for a few metres to a stile immediately to the left of a house leading into woodland by the riverside. This soon crosses two stiles and follows pasture along the River Wharfe through Low Park – part of the Dales Way, the popular 81 mile route that links the Yorkshire Dales and the Lake District from Ilkley to Windermere. There are fine views both across the riverside and back to Ilkley Moor, with its twin summit wireless masts a notable landmark ahead.

The path crosses two more stiles before climbing wooden steps and emerging on the road by Fairfield House where the next section of route immediately starts, again going along the riverside. At High Mill continue past the caravan site and the old textile mill itself, now converted to riverside homes. The path climbs to the suspension bridge and Bark Lane. Anyone heading for the centre of Addingham for refreshment, toilets and public transport should turn left; but then go first right along Church Lane to Main Street and the village centre.

Bolton Priory

A famous walk by one of England's most beautiful ecclesiastical ruins, too fine to omit from any book of walks in Upper Wharfedale, particularily recommended in the winter months when the return riverside walk is less likely to be shared with lines of parked cars.

Distance: 2½ miles   Time required: 1½-2 hours

Terrain: Easy woodland and riverside paths.

Parking: Large public car park at Bolton Abbey on the B6160 road from Ilkley and Addingham.

Public Transport: Weekday services from Skipton and Grassington Bus Stations (service 76); weekend Dalesbus services from Leeds and Ilkley (Dalesbus 800), plus limited Sunday services from certain Lancashire towns – Leisurelink.

Refreshment: Bolton Abbey – snack bar in car park; cafe at post office; cafeteria with choice of meals and snacks at Cavendish Pavilion – half way point.

Map: OS Outdoor Leisure Yorkshire Dales (Sheet 10 Southern area); OS Pathfinder SE05/15 Bolton Abbey and Blubberhouses. Stile Maps: Bolton Abbey Footpath Map.

FROM the Bolton Abbey car park make your way to the top and out by the information board and refreshment kiosk (toilets nearby). Bear right along the lane to the main road where, opposite the junction, the "hole in the wall" gateway leads to that first magnificent view of Bolton Priory in its setting on a buff of land within a great arc of the river.

Go down the steps and along the path – but if you choose to visit the priory before the walk (you pass it again on the return journey) branch left to the stile in the fence which runs alongside the main drive down to the priory church.

Though the village is known as Bolton Abbey, the famous ruins set in such immaculate parkland are actually the surviving portions of an Augustinian priory, dating from the 12th century. They contain work right up to the 16th century when Prior Richard Moone was forced to surrender his community to Thomas Cromwell on 29th January

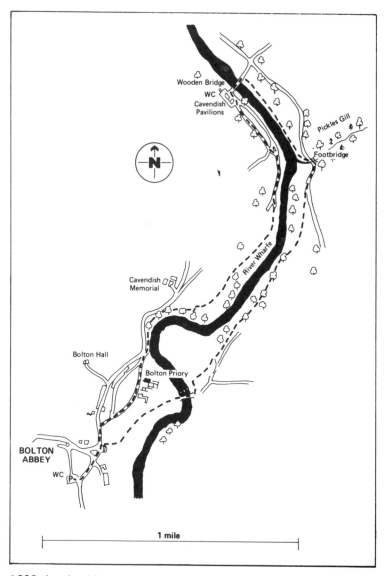

Wooden Bridge
WC
Cavendish
Pavilions
Pickles Gill
Footbridge

N

River Wharfe

Cavendish
Memorial

Bolton Hall

Bolton Priory

BOLTON
ABBEY
WC P

1 mile

1539, leaving his great west tower, which forms the entrance to the church, unfinished.

Fortunately, the beautiful priory church survives and continues, as it has for many centuries, as the parish church for the village community of Bolton Abbey. It welcomes thousands of visitors each year – local guides are on duty at busy times and will explain architectural and other details.

The splendours of the ancient church and its associated ruins have attracted enthusiasts of the picturesque for over two hundred years, among them such giants of the English Romantic movement as the poet Wordsworth, the painters Girtin, Cox, Turner and Landseer and the Victorian art critic and moralist John Ruskin.

Bolton Abbey has also, for successive generations, been the focal point of the Yorkshire estates of the Dukes of Devonshire, and the great and famous, including prime ministers and monarchs (King George V was a frequent guest) have stayed in the handsome Gothic shooting lodge converted from the gatehouse, opposite the priory.

When you have had time throughly to explore the priory church and ruins, make your way through the little gate to the far side of the graveyard and walk down to cross the footbridge (or parallel stepping stones) across the River Wharfe. At the other side, take the path which bears slightly to the right, up steps.

Keep on the main path which follows the hillside into the Priory Woods – ignoring the path, signed to Storiths, which zigzags to the right.

There are magnificent views back to the priory ruins from here with, if the river runs calmly, fine reflections in the water. The paths through the woods have recently been restored. They were originally laid out as ornamental walks for visitors around 150 years ago by a remarkable vicar of Bolton Abbey – the Reverend William Carr, a noted scholar whose claims to fame included the first ever Yorkshire dialect dictionary and the breeding of the oversized "Craven Heifer", which is still to be seen in local inn signs.

Keep on along the main path which follows a man-made shelf through the woods before emerging at the lane above Pickles Gill – a footbridge across the beck here will save you getting wet feet in the ford.

A stile in the wall corner to the left gives access to the riverside path leading to the recently restored wooden bridge at Cavendish Pavilion – a welcoming cafeteria which is open for most of the year including winter weekends. There are toilets nearby.

You can, if you've time and energy, more than double the length of this walk by following one of a choice of waymarked trails through Strid Woods (entrance by the pavilion), continuing as far as Barden Tower. An admission ticket to the woods also buys a map of the trails.

The route back is along the drive up from the Cavendish Pavilion but almost immediately bears left to the riverside. Keep along by the river for about half a mile, past the end of the car park, before bearing right to where a steep path, with steps, leads out of the field corner and to the entrance of the Pavilion drive on the B6160, next to the Gothic fountain. This was built as a memorial to Lord Frederick Cavendish, heir to the Devonshire estates, who was murdered by Irish nationalists in Phoenix Park, Dublin, in 1882.

Continue ahead to where the path, parallel to the road, crosses a wooden footbridge over a ravine, and leads to the gate and entrance to Bolton Priory from the opposite side. Continue past the Priory and along the drive, taking the stile in the fence, left, which leads back up to the "hole in the wall" and the car park.

Halton Heights

A walk on the edge of Barden Moor offering some magnificent high-level views of the dale, returning by field path, specially recommended in late summer when the heather on the moors is a rich shade of purple.

Distance: 4½ miles   Time required: 3 hours

Terrain: Rough moorland tracks and field paths and a steady uphill climb of half a mile at the end of the walk. Boots advised. Because of the nature of the start of the walk across open country, it is not recommended in times of poor visibility such as mist or low cloud.

Parking:Free informal parking places at Halton Heights just past the cattle grid on the Skipton-Embsay-Barden road. From Skipton follow Embsay signs and continue beyond Eastby to Halton Heights. From the B6160 Addingham-Burnsall road turn left just before Barden Tower to reach the car park on the summit of the hill.

Public Transport: Service 76 from Skipton bus station to Eastby – start the walk at Eastby. (More frequent service to and from Embsay, one mile from Eastby, by service 75).

Refreshment: Eastby (Inn)

Maps: OS Outdoor Leisure Sheet 10 (Yorkshire Dales Southern Area); OS Pathfinder SE05/15 Bolton Abbey and Blubberhouses.

BARDEN Moor and Fell constitute one of the finest areas of unspoiled heather moorland in the North of England to which there is legal public access. However the moor is closed on certain days of the year for shooting between August and December – never on Sundays – and at times of high fire risk. Though this walk largely uses public rights-of-way on the moor, it is not advisable to do this walk at such times – notices are posted on the moor to warn walkers. Dogs are not permitted on the moor, but if dog owners take care to keep strictly to the rights-of-way as shown on the Outdoor Leisure or Pathfinder Map and keep their dog under control, they are perfectly within their rights on the public path.

From the car park, head along the obvious stony track which starts just west of the cattle grid (the right-of-way begins another 100 metres

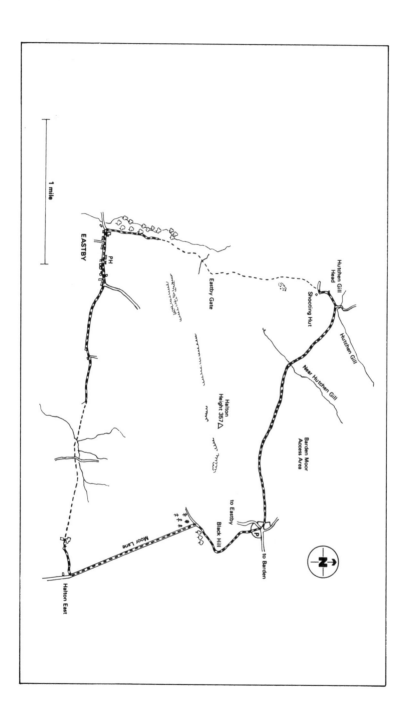

EASTBY

PH

Eastby Gate

Hutchen Gill Head

Shooting Hut

Hutchen Gill

Near Hutchen Gill

Halton Height 357 △

Barden Moor Access Area

Moor Lane

Black Hill

to Eastby

to Barden

P

Halton East

1 mile

N

to the south) and bear westwards over the moor. This is a fairly level way soon giving quite splendid views across Lower Barden Reservoir and an area of desolately beautiful heather landscape, stretching away across a great, empty bowl to the summit of the moor. You'll hear the angry chatter of grouse swooping up from clumps of heather at most times hovering above a rocky outcrop looking for lizards or voles.

The track, which is joined by the right-of-way, soon swings round along the contour — avoid a fainter track forking off left but keep on the main way which crosses a stream, near Hutchen Gill, then curves round to a deeper little ravine, Hutchen Gill itself. Just before the gill, a track bears left towards a shooting hut. This is not the public path which only branches off a faint and narrow way some 200 metres to the north. But unless you've a dog with you, most people will prefer the obvious short cut to the shooting hut (strictly private) at Hutchen Gill Head.

Turn left at the hut to locate a narrow path which follows the top of a narrow dyke, east of the shooting butts, heading due south across the moorland. Again this more obvious and better used route diverts slightly from the right-of-way. Head just to the right of the line of crags – Eastby Crag – you will see ahead. A large plantation forms a further landmark to the left, with the more spectacular conical summit of Embsay Crag further to the right.

The path peters out in moorland grass, but you should be able to see a gate and ladder stile ahead – Eastby Gate – which leads off the moor.

Cross the stile and you enter an enclosed green lane with further stiles ahead, bearing slightly right. There are fine views from here across the narrow shoulder of land which separates Wharfedale and Airedale, crossed by the main A59 and A65 roads by Draughton. Haw Pikes quarries are to the left and, if it happens to be a Sunday, Embsay Steam Railway's little steam locomotive with its trailing coaches is clearly in view as it puffs along to Holywell Halt. Keep ahead, your way marked by stiles, down a little ravine, Heigh Gill. The path soon crosses a stile to enter a wood, extremely picturesque if somewhat muddy, with a little waterfall to your right.

You emerge by cottages into the lane at Eastby – turn left along the main street, past the village pub, but where the road swings left towards Barden, keep directly ahead along Bark Lane, an unmetalled track. Continue, through gates, as the way becomes a pleasant field path beyond the evocatively named barn, Angrymire Laithe. Keep in the same direction, the path going along the edge of fields, the way now marked by stiles, soon crossing Berry Ground Beck at a little footbridge and following the far side of the stream over more stiles.

You soon find yourself in a large open field – head towards a stile slightly to the right and towards the farm ahead. Go through a gate at the farm, turning right through and between farm buildings then left on to the main farm drive – closing gates behind you. The farm drive brings you to a cross roads. Turn left here, into Moor Lane, a broad green way which as it names implies is an ancient access way to the moor.

You have a steady uphill climb now, but take time to pause and catch your breath and turn back to enjoy impressive views across Draughton and Skipton Moor. At the top gate follow the track to the right, round the edge of Black Hill, to car parks below Halton Height.

Thorpe in the Hollow

This is a favourite walk between two of the most perfectly situated villages in Upper Wharfedale, along paths that offer exceptionally fine views.

Distance: 3½ miles   Time required: 2 hours

Terrain: Field paths and a section of riverside. Quite a number of stiles to negotiate – not a walk to be hurried.

Parking: In the public car park by the riverside at Burnsall.

Public Transport: Service 76 from Skipton or from Grassington bus station to Burnsall (weekdays only). Service 800 (Dalesbus) at weekends April-October, direct from Ilkley, Bradford and Leeds.

Refreshment: Burnsall – choice of cafes and two inns. Toilets by the car park.

Maps: OS Outdoor Leisure Sheet 10: Yorkshire Dales (Southern Area); OS Pathfinder SE06/16 Grassington and Pateley Bridge. Stile Maps: Grassington Footpath Map.

IT IS difficult to imagine a better setting for a village than Burnsall enjoys – where the River Wharfe, having been forced into a deep limestone ravine, opens out into a green and sheltered south-facing valley, protected on all sides by 1,500 feet high fells. The village has a medieval church with two Anglo-Viking "hog-back" gravestones, a 17th century, Grammar School now used as the local primary school, a riverside village green complete with maypole, and a scatter of cottages and small houses which create a perfect harmony with the wild fell country all around. The handsome bridge was last rebuilt in the 19th century, after being destroyed by floods. Following a similar occurrence in the 17th century the bill was paid by Sir William Craven, the "Dick Whittington of the Dales" who left his native Appletreewick eventually to become Lord mayor of London. As well as restoring the bridge, he rebuilt the church and built and endowed the Grammar School.

From Burnsall car park walk to the crossroads by the Red Lion, keeping left along the Grassington road, following the road as it bears sharp right. Just past the corner, by a stone horse trough, a gate by a

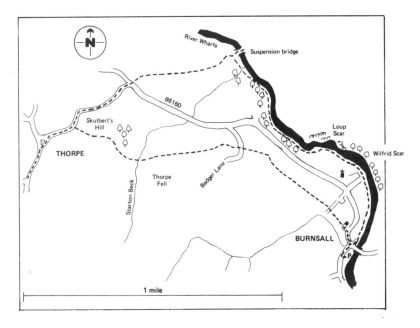

wooden footpath sign leads across a small stone flagged yard to another gate. Go through both by the edge of a garden to a stile leading into a field.

The path is now marked by a series of low step stiles across the fields, some with little lambing gates above them. Notice how the stiles are of a darker sandstone contrasting to the pale limestone of the rest of the walls. This is because the path lies close to the major fault lines where the newer darker sandstones yield to the paler Great Scar limestones giving a pepper-and-salt effect to the walls.

Keep ahead through stiles across a farmtrack and over more stiles through small fields. To your left rises the massive bulk of Thorpe Fell – part of the Barden Moor Access Area – forming an impressive skyline.

Soon after the path crosses another farmtrack you find yourself in a broader field, close to a line of wooden pylons, with a triangular section of drystone wall ahead of you. Keep to the right of the apex of this triangle to locate a stile a few yards to the right. The way now crosses another farmtrack, Badger lane, and along a wall – fine views to the right across the valley to the village of Hebden with its church. As the path dips, look for a signpost near the wall indicating the way which now bears left up the pasture, close to two ash trees, dipping

25

down again to a ladder stile. Cross to the next stile, the way now descending to a little plank bridge over a stream, Starton Beck. Follow the way up by the wall which encloses a small wood, going through a gate and bearing slightly left to a ladder stile. This enters a green lane.

Follow this to the junction with the metalled lane into Thorpe.

Thorpe in the Hollow, or Thorpe-sub-montem to give it its latinate name, was known as the hidden village because according to legend it escaped the depredations of 14th century Scottish raiders. They reputedly passed down the dale not knowing of the village's existence, situated as it is in a tight hollow of the hills. In medieval times it was reputed to be a centre of shoemakers – a cobbler was at work here up until about a century ago.

Little else has changed here since last century, and as you arrive in the village there's a magnificent 18th century farmhouse on your right and two handsome barns, with neo-classical features, on the left. The road through the village becomes a track and then a moorland path over the shoulder of Elbolton Hill with its caves where a number of important archaeological finds were made in the last century.

To return to Burnsall, retrace your steps along the lane out of Thorpe, but keep ahead over the brow of the hill past the point where the green lane branches off, soon dropping down into the main valley towards the main road. The views are extensive – to the right you'll see Grass Wood and beyond Old Cote Moor, Buckden Pike and Great Whernside, Grassington Moor and, just discernible above Hebden Gill, Grassington Moor Lead Mines' Chimney. The crag above the felltop to the south west is Simons Seat.

At the main road cross immediately to a ladder stile and a bridleway signed to Hebden. Follow the wall to another stile, descending now to a gateway marked with blue bridleway waymarks, and follow a line of posts taking you down to the little suspension bridge over the Wharfe, leading to Hebden below. This bridge was made just over 100 years ago by the local blacksmith who constructed the bridge in pieces for it to be erected on site and tensioned by wires – a quite remarkable achievement.

Do not cross but turn left along a quite superb stretch of sheltered path by the river Wharfe – part of the Dales Way. Soon across a stile and a little footbridge the Way follows the river past Loup Scar, a high crag of exposed limestone, climbing a little grassy knoll before returning to the riverside where mallards and the occasional swan are to be seen. Another fine limestone escarpment is passed before coming into the village behind the Red Lion inn car park. You can return to the car park by going down steps at and under the bridge, crossing riverside cobbles to make your way back up the little embankment and on to the village green. There are few nicer ways to end a walk.

Linton and Threshfield

A walk from Grassington to take in two attractive neighbouring villages – Threshfield and Linton – with opportunity to enjoy some unusually fine views of this historic landscape.

Distance: 4 miles   Time required: 2-2½ hours

Terrain: Field paths and tracks. Two short uphill sections. Boots advised – some places can be muddy after rain.

Parking: In the National Park car park on Hebden Road (Pateley Bridge road) out of Grassington. Alternative car park available on the road to Linton Church – this shortens the walk by half a mile.

Public Transport: Service 71 or 72 from Skipton bus station to Grassington; Service 800 (Dalesbus) at weekends April-October from Ilkley, Bradford and Leeds.

Refreshment: Grassington – choice of cafes and inns. Toilets by National Park centre. Public houses in both Threshfield and Linton.

Maps: OS Outdoor Leisure Sheet 10: (Yorkshire Dales Southern area); OS Pathfinder SE06/16 Grassington and Pateley Bridge. Stile Maps: Grassington Footpath Map.

FROM the National Park car park and visitor centre, walk across to the far south corner where a wooden kissing gate leads to an enclosed and paved footpath. This is locally known for self-evident reasons as the "Snake Walk" which winds down, through another pedestrian gate, to Linton Falls.

These spectacular falls across the Great Scar limestone mark the point where one of the branches of the Craven Fault – an area of geological fracture – crosses the Wharfe valley. One feature of this walk is the contrast between the paler limestone rocks in the riverside area and the dark, brooding gritstone crags of the high moorland.

For many centuries a watermill existed on his spot, and a former textile mill – Linton Mill – was recently demolished to make way for the new housing development across the river.

Cross the narrow footbridge known as the "Tin Bridge" after an earlier, metal plated structure – the present bridge was recently

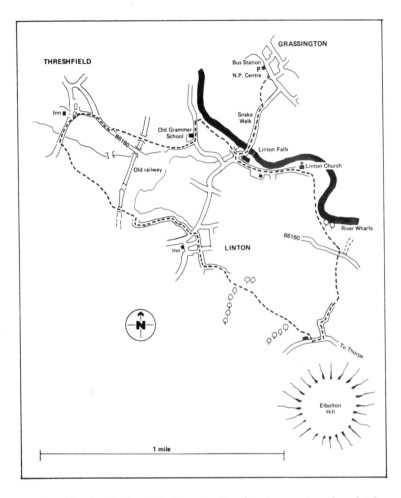

replaced by the National Park authority after the previous iron lattice bridge became dangerous. Turn left across the bridge by the houses to the tiny hump-back bridge over Captain Beck – another important former mill stream – to follow the path upstream across the field which soon goes to a short section of wooded riverside. The old brick building on the right by the riverside was, until the 1950s, a hydro-electric station which supplied Grassington with electric power.

The path skirts woodland and emerges into the lane from Linton Church. Turn left here, soon passing the little 17th century Threshfield Grammar School, still in use as the local primary school. Immediately past the school is a field gate on the right. This leads to a footpath

29

along a grassy track which climbs uphill by the wall, soon bearing right to another gate and over the railway bridge which crosses the disused Yorkshire Dales Railway. Though it closed in 1931 to passenger traffic, the line remained in use until the late 1960s for freight and excursion trains. It still exists as far as the Tilcon Quarry at Swinden with daily trains to steel and cement works.

Continue along the grassy track to the main road at a field gate, turn right to the crossroads and then left along the line into the centre of Threshfield.

Set back behind a busy crossroads, Threshfield is a village which most people go through without stopping or confuse with the spread of surburbia along the main Grassington road. It does have an old centre and little village green surrounded by old cottages and a Manor House which dates from the 17th century, as well as a village inn, The Old Hall.

Unless you are visiting the inn, turn left before the green and walk down to the main road, past the manor house and a barn with its door displaying a rich variety of local horseshoes, to the bridge over the stream. Some 50 metres uphill on the left is a stile. Go through and climb the field to the wall corner where another path is joined by the wallside. Keep left to the next stile, then over the old footbridge over the non-existent railway, before joining a narrow track to Linton. The handsome house on the left linked by stepping stones on the far side of Captain Beck is White Abbey, the former home of the celebrated Dales novelist and topographer Halliwell Sutcliffe.

Linton is one of the most beautiful of all Dales villages. It has a large village green around which the village is situated, crossed by a stream, road, ford and footbridges. The handsome neo-classical building at the far end of the green, reputedly built to the design of the great Sir John Vanbrugh, is Fountains Hospital, an almshouse for local pensioners which is still maintained by the endowment of Richard Fountain, who was born in Linton and became a wealthy alderman of London where he died in 1725.

Also overlooking the green is the white-walled Fountain Inn, whilst a number of houses and cottages by the green, in quiet side roads and along the main road, all date from the 17th and 18th centuries. Many have the characteristic mullioned windows and dripstones that were used in the conservative-minded Yorkshire Dales well into the 18th century. Not suprisingly the village is a Conservation Area.

The way continues by crossing the footbridge to the far side of the stream and along to the far end of the village where a farmtrack, left, goes between buildings. The path follows the wall uphill – ignore a ladder stile on the left, but make for the stile ahead. Continue uphill past a narrow section of woodland to the next stile. Then go across a field to a stile immediately to the left of a barn which leads into a narrow lane.

You are now on the side of Elbolton Hill, one of the seven hills of Linton – all of them reef knolls, a rare geological phenomenon consisting of pure deposited limestone, so pure than one of them across the valley, Swinden, has now been totally quarried away for limestone extraction. The views across the valley towards Grassington, Hebden and Grassington Moor are particularly fine. The shallow green terraces visible on the hillside around you and as you begin to descend are raines or lynchets; ancient cultivation terraces which date from Anglian times and mark where arable crops – mainly oats – where grown in terraced fields like modern vineyards.

Turn left in the lane but after about 60 metres a small bridle gate on the left gives access to a beautiful little enclosed bridleway leading down the hillside – this can be overgrown – between walls. Where it ends at a gate, keep slightly left down across the pasture to a gate ahead. A second gate ahead leads to the main road.

Cross with care. Almost immediately to the right is a stile and a further path which bears left through a series of three narrow stiles before entering a large open field, a grassy terrace above the river Wharfe. You see Linton Church below. A ladder stile over the wall below and to the right crosses to a path leading directly to Linton Church, joining a path to a stile and a way through the churchyard.

Linton Church, with its little bell tower, dates from the 11th century and is exceptionally interesting in terms of its many Norman and 14th century features. As the ancient parish church of the whole of this part of the dale, it probably occupies a prehistoric site. It has played a major role in the life of the dale over the best part of the last millenium and has many features of exceptional interest. If you visit the church (make sure your boots are clean) you will find a guide on sale.

The road from the church passes the alternative car park and a row of former mill cottages known for reasons which are not entirely certain as "Botany" – probably a link with "Botany Bay" where people were once banished, an ironic reference to the distance people had to walk from Grassington or Linton.

Immediately past the new houses, a passageway leads to the "Tin Bridge" and the "Snake Walk" back to Grassington.

Grassington and Hebden

A walk between two popular Dales villages taking advantage of less well-known footpaths that offer some unexpected and interesting views of the upper dale.

Distance: 4 miles   Time required: 2-2½ hours.

Terrain: Pasture and small enclosures with numerous stiles. One short uphill section. Boots advised – some places can be muddy after rain.

Parking: In the National Park car park on Hebden Road (Pateley Bridge road) out of Grassington.

Public Transport: Service 71 or 72 from Skipton bus station to Grassington; Service 800 (Dalesbus at weekends April-October from Ilkley, Bradford and Leeds.

Refreshment: Grassington – choice of cafes and inns. Toilets at National Park centre. Hebden – The Clarendon Inn. Toilets at far end of village.

Maps: OS Outdoor Leisure Sheet 10: (Yorkshire Dales Southern area): OS Pathfinder SE06/16 Grassington and Pateley Bridge. Stile Maps: Grassington Footpath Map.

GRASSINGTON, the unofficial capital of Upper Wharfedale, is an excellent starting point for a walk and has a great deal to explore in its own right. You might start your walk by picking up a copy of the Grassington Village Trail from the National Park Centre or local shops, it explains much of the fascinating history of this former lead-mining community.

To begin the main walk, from the National Park Centre go along Hebden Road towards the village centre, turning right into the Square and continuing up Main Street past shops and cafes to the top Square by the Town Hall – the former Mechanics' Institute and still a focal point of the life of the village.

Go right in front of the Town Hall along Low Lane, soon branching left at Garrs End into High Lane – signposted for Hebden. This ancient, sunken track was once an important route to Hebden used by packhorse traffic as its old name "Horse Gap Yett" still indicates. It

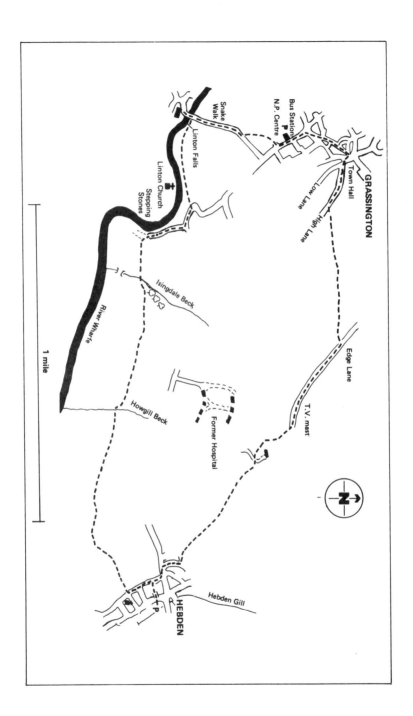

GRASSINGTON

Town Hall

Bus Station
N.P. Centre

Snake Walk

Linton Falls

Linton Church

Stepping Stones

Low Lane

High Lane

Edge Lane

T.V. mast

River Wharfe

Isingdale Beck

Howgill Beck

Former Hospital

Hebden Gill

HEBDEN

N

1 mile

climbs up and bears right, behind the village, and you are soon looking across rooftops into the valley beyond. After about 200 metres from the junction a metal field gate, about 10 metres before a thorn tree on the left, gives access to a field path not visible on the ground. This crosses to a step stile in the wall on the right, some 30 metres from the wall corner.

Your way is now diagonally across a number of fields, climbing in the direction of the television booster mast you will see ahead, and the one after is in the top right hand corner of the field, with the next immediately behind it. Two more stiles follow, relatively easy to find, before you join a high level enclosed track – Edge Lane – at a gate.

Turn right here, continuing to climb gently uphill towards the television mast. The views are magnificent in every direction – to the north-west, behind you, you'll see Old Cote Moor and Littondale; to the south-west the quarries and the great reef knolls towards Cracoe, then the great expanse of Thorpe Fell and Burnsall Moor (forming part of the Barden Moor Access Area). Ahead of you, as you complete the ascent, is Barden Fell and Simons Seat with the village of Hebden coming into view as you come over the brow of the hill.

Soon past the television mast is a gate and a ladder stile on the right. Cross, descending the pasture above the former Grassington Isolation Hospital, over a little stile ahead and towards a pine wood. The path goes through the edge of the wood to a stile and crossing of paths. Bear left, signed to Hebden, over the stile, going in front of Garnshaw House farm to the stile in the next wall ahead. Again a crossing path, and again you make for Hebden, this time descending through the middle of a broad pasture towards a gap ahead leading to a path which descends by a wall to another stile. The path now bears right across the centre of a long field; make directly for the farm and village ahead. At the bottom of the field a gate leads into a track to a lane. Turn right to reach the main Grassington road by Hargreaves bus garage. The Clarendon Hotel is immediately to your left, as is the village centre around its attractive gill.

Otherwise cross and almost immediately opposite is Brayshaw Lane which leads round the back of this former mining village. Continue to Hebden's little Victorian parish church.

The path back to Grassington begins at the field gate opposite the church and is a historic route – being the ancient parishioners' way from the village to Linton Church used by the people of Hebden before their own church was built in the last century. It is also an exceptionally pretty route with grand views not only of Thorpe Fell and Barden Moor, now seen so clearly in profile, but down into the deep river gorge of the River Wharfe carved out by its ancient glacier.

Your path is in the far right-hand corner of the field, through the farthest of the two gates by a solitary tree. Go along the wall to a steep step stile in the wall corner ahead, then along the wall over another stile as you climb uphill, crossing a narrow pasture to a gap stile. Go right here alongside a ruined wall along another narrow field. Continue alongside the next section of ruined wall ahead to a narrow stile.

Now follow a series of stiles of almost every conceivable type – gap or "squeezer" stiles, step stiles, ladder stiles, little gates – as the path, older than the fields it crosses, follows a high terrace above the river. Just about opposite the end of the former hospital the path, well signed, dog-legs right and then left before following a fence to cross a stream, Howgill Beck, by a welcome National Park boardwalk and footbridge. As you enter open pasture, head for the yellow marker post and the little barn, Ray Laithe, ahead, dropping to another stile though the wall concealed in the hollow. Head to the left of the barn, about 10 metres below which a stile leads to a path which swings left above the wooded Isingdale Beck to another stile.

Cross, bearing right over a little footbridge, and follow the wall, heading towards the riverside. The ancient parishoners' way actually crossed the stepping stones to the 12th century Linton Church, but you'll probably prefer to keep dry feet and go over the stile on the right and along Mill Lane, past Grassington's medieval corn mill (now converted for residential use) and the trout farm. Look at the powerful underground spring at the far side of the farm which drains from Grassington Moor and once powered the furnace bellows of an 18th century lead smeltmill situated at this point.

The path back to Grassington starts from the stile on the left some 50 metres above the trout farm, and again follows a low terrace above the river. Keep ahead at the next stile to the stile by the "Tin Bridge" at Linton Falls – an attractive natural gorge where the Wharfe crosses the limestone outcrops of the Craven Fault. Turn right into the narrow enclosed path known as the "Snake Walk" to the car park and Grassington village.

Grass Wood

Grass Wood is that rare jewel – a semi-natural wood on limestone, one of the most beautiful small woods of its kind in the North of England and a nature reserve of national importance.

Distance: 4 miles   Time required: 2-2½ hours

Terrain: Woodland and riverside paths and tracks. One short uphill section. Boots advised – some places can be muddy after rain.

Parking: In the National Park car park on Hebden Road (Pateley Bridge road) out of Grassington.

Public Transport: Service 71 or 72 from Skipton bus station to Grassington; Service 800 (Dalesbus) at weekends April-October from Ilkley, Bradford and Leeds.

Refreshment: Grassington – choice of cafes and inns. Toilets by National Park Centre.

Maps: OS Outdoor Leisure Sheet 10: (Yorkshire Dales Southern area); OS Pathfinder SE06/16 Grassington and Pateley Bridge. Stile Maps: Grassington Footpath Map.

FROM the National Park Centre (opposite the bus station) turn left in Hebden Road towards Grassington village but at the crossroads keep ahead along Wood Lane, passing Grassington Old Hall on your right – a private house but the oldest inhabited building in Wharfedale, dating back to the 18th century.

Continue along Wood Lane. After about 80 metres, turn left into the road known as Raines Meadow, along a road by a new housing estate. As the road bends sharply left, look for steps straight ahead decending to Raines Lane below. Cross and keep ahead to a narrow way by gardens through a kissing gate, crossing a small field to a stile in the wall corner by the end of Grassington Bridge – a low grassy area with a bench, know locally as Donkey Hill.

Don't go up to the road but turn immediately right along the farm track to a kissing gate. This leads to a path that crosses the meadowland to the riverside. Follow the river upstream, soon crossing a stile in the wall and then a little footbridge over a stream. This is a particularily lovely stretch of riverside with the white waters

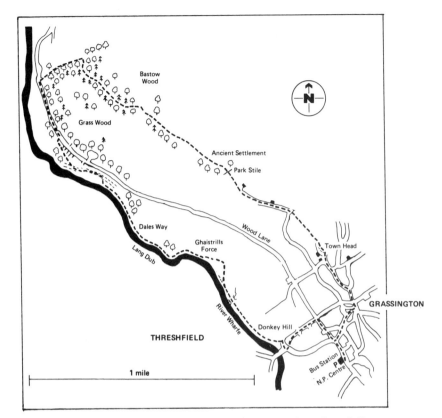

of the Wharfe making a vividly beautiful series of shallow falls set against a backcloth of pale limestone crags and thin woodland.

Follow the path slightly to the right over two step stiles, moving slightly away from the riverside as the path goes along the top of a shallow cliff, with the river in an area of rapids below.

Your way climbs around this little ravine before, at a further ladder stile, entering an expanse of open woodland, grazed by sheep. To the left the river is now in a deep gorge, the surrounding rocks carved and polished smooth with the action of the water. This is Ghaistrills Strid, very much less fearful a place than the Strid at Bolton Abbey, but nonetheless to be treated with respect as the river courses through deep, fast flowing channels. The name "Ghaistrills" is a mystery but is thought to refer to the ghostly sound made by the water through the rapids.

Yet only a few metres further on as you follow the path round, the river is calm, broad and still, often whisky brown in colour above its pebbly bed, from the peaty moors and fellsides from where it drains. This is a good place for wildlife if there aren't too many visitors around with dogs, boats and stone-throwing children – dippers in the pools, swallows skimming the water, and if you're lucky perhaps even a kingfisher giving a vivid flash of brilliant colour as he darts across the banks.

Make your way carefully down the rocky path to the riverside and continue alongside the river to a stile and narrow pasture to re-enter the wood. The path now bears away from and above the steep sides of the river which here forms a series of deep dark pools known as Black Dubs – "dub" being local dialect for pools.

Keep in the same direction through a lovely area of scattered oak and birch wood, a good place to see the odd primrose or wood anemone in spring. As the wood thins away, bear right away from the river towards the gate and a step stile into Wood Lane. Go left into Wood Lane for about 100 metres before turning right at a stile and gate into Grass Wood Nature Reserve.

Please keep to the main path through this Reserve, owned and managed by Wharfedale Naturalists' Trust, to help reduce trampling and damage, for this is a woodland of national importance for its wildflowers. Among the more common to be seen in the late spring and early summer are primroses, cowslips, wood anemone, bluebell, bird's eye primrose, false oxlips, lily of the valley and several species of orchid. It goes without saying that it is illegal to pick wildflowers in the wood and care should be taken at all times to avoid leaving litter or doing anything that could remotely cause a fire. In addition to wild flowers, there are a wide variety of native trees including such lovely specimens as bird cherry, blackthorn, guelder rose, yew, hazel, Scots pine and many more, as well as plantations of larch, spruce and beech. Bird life is also particularily rich including nuthatch, willow warblers, finches and the occasional woodpecker.

The track climbs steadily uphill through the woodland. After about 200 metres there is a clear junction of tracks. Take the waymarked route to the right, still uphill. This is not the actual line of the public right-of-way as on the Ordnance Map but is easier to follow and Trust wardens prefer this path to be used. A steady uphill ascent now, but with fine views between the trees as you ascend. At the summit keep on the main path, avoiding crossing paths. You now begin to descend into a rocky, thickly wooded gorge.

Keep the same direction, through dense, dark woodland, following a clear, stony path until it levels out and you see ahead a green sign indicating the site of a prehistoric (Celtic) village – a settlement of the ancient Brigantes who occupied this part of Grass Wood and nearby village field settlements, probably well on into Roman times. These Roman British settlements pre-dated the present village of Grassington which, as is name implies, is an Anglian settlement probably near the ancient enclosures or "ings" created by the Brigantes.

You are directed round the edge of the prehistoric site until you reach a wall and steep stile, Park Stile, ahead. Cross. Your path is almost directly ahead but to the right of the wall and barn ahead. Make for a field gate where the path enters a broad and usually muddy lane by a barn. As the lane bears right, look for a stile by steps in the wall corner – this climbs at the corner of a field.

Climb this field and keep the same direction towards the wall with a gap stile straight ahead. Go through here, making your way to the farm ahead, the path following a concrete track, almost always muddy, round the outside of the cow house and through the farm gate into Chapel Street, Grassington.

Continue along Chapel Street past Town Head, a beautiful 17th century yeoman farmer's house with stone mullioned windows. The cottages on the left as you walk further down Chapel Street are typical lead miners' cottages, and probably contained families of five or six in appalling overcrowded conditions during the height of the mines' prosperity in the early years of last century.

You arrive at Grassington Town Hall with its handsome clock. At the little Square there is a choice of ways back through the village. Perhaps rather than going down the Main Street on the right, take the stony track immediately down to the left of the cottages ahead – this leads to Pletts' Barn, a magnificent 18th century barn where John Wesley himself once preached. It is now specialising in walking equipment and on the first floor is Waymarks, a small interpretive centre where walkers are always welcome.

Kettlewell and Starbotton

This walk uses a lovely stretch of the Dales Way and returns along an elevated limestone terrace with exceptional views of this steeply glaciated section of valley.

Distance: 4¼ miles   Time required: 2-2½ hours.

Terrain: Paths and tracks by riverside and across pasture. Fairly level – but a number of stiles to cross.

Parking: In the National Park car park at Kettlewell.

Public Transport: Service 71 from Skipton bus station to Kettlewell; Service 800 (Dalesbus) at weekends April-October from Ilkley, Bradford and Leeds.

Refreshment: Kettlewell – choice of cafes and inns. Toilets in the village. Pub at Starbotton.

Maps: OS Outdoor Leisure No 30: Yorkshire Dales (North and Central); Stile Maps: The Dales Way Route Guide.

FROM Kettlewell bridge take the path through the gateway at the far side of the bridge, soon bearing right with the signpost down to the riverside and a kissing gate. You will soon be walking along one of several sections of this path which have been stabilised by the National Park authority to counteract the erosive effect of the river and human feet.

This path, well-used, is easy to follow and clear on the ground, waymarked in places, as well as being clearly indicated by stiles and gates.

You go through a second kissing gate, the path veering away from the river, soon going along an enclosed, stony track past a large barn. Cross open fields, then back into an enclosed way. Ladder stiles and usually adjacent gates mark the way.

Notice how steep the valley sides are – a superb example of a U-shaped glaciated valley, the steep sides carved out by the great Wharfedale glacier in the last Ice Age. Note, too, the ridges in the field – these are "raines" or "lynchets", remnants of ancient terraced

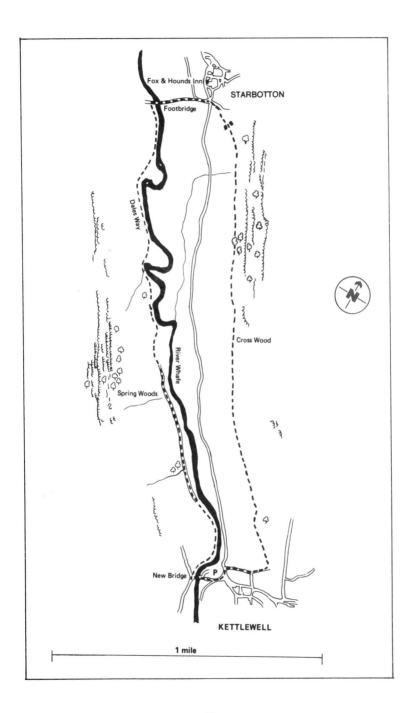

Fox & Hounds Inn

STARBOTTON

Footbridge

Dales Way

River Whafe

Cross Wood

Spring Woods

New Bridge   P

KETTLEWELL

1 mile

41

arable field. They were in use from Anglian times until the early 19th century, mainly for growing oats, the staple fare of the Dales for many centuries. There are also some attractive areas of semi-natural woodland clinging to the steep slopes.

More ladder stiles and the path bears right close to a great bend in the river, which loops away and then is rejoined by the path as it loops back. This is another resurfaced section of path. Keep ahead across a tiny footbridge, then over a field and a little complex of stiles to reach the footbridge across the River Wharfe and an enclosed, stony way which takes you into the edge of Starbotton.

The unusual name of this settlement probably means a stony valley but could also indicate a place where standards – poles – were cut. It is a village of attractive stone cottages and houses which date from the 17th century, but the 20th century examples, in local material and traditional style, blend well with the old – a tribute to the National Park planners.

If you seek refreshment, the Fox and Hounds Inn on the main road at the far end of the village is a typical small, stone-floored Dales pub, welcoming walkers. Otherwise cross the road, turning right and then first left where, below a drive from cottages, a path, signposted, bears right through a gate. Follow the green way through gateways. The path on the Ordnance Map is shown as going sharp left up the narrow pasture to the rickety gate above, but the path most walkers use and clearly the farmers prefer to be used, is through the next gate and behind the barn ahead where a gate rejoins the original path. Follow the wall along to a pedestrian gate in the wall corner.

This path is easier to follow, from now on clearly visible on the ground and indicated by ladder stiles throughout. You soon begin to ascend slightly, following a natural limestone terrace above narrow enclosures to the right, with increasingly fine views down and across the valley with river and road below you. The path goes along the edge of a wood, mainly beech and gnarled thorn clinging to the hillside. Follow the way as it curves round a shallow ravine, over a shallow beck, then finds its way back into open pasture. Step stiles over the many crossing walls mark the way. You pass another small wood, Cross Wood, the path now veering towards the wallside to your right, above the lower pastures with their scattered barns.

Soon Kettlewell comes into view, clustered below the great bluff of Middlesmoor Scars under which the main road to Skipton climbs. The path enters another little wood by a wooden step stile, then follows the wall round as it curves to the right, to go through a little stile and gate into a narrow enclosure by houses.

You'll find yourself in Kettlewell's back lane – ahead to pubs, cafes and car park.

Cray Gill and Hubberholme

This classic walk at the head of Upper Wharfedale and into Langstrothdale offers some outstanding views and is rich in historical interest.

Distance: 4 miles   Time required: 2-2½ hours

Terrain: Paths and tracks across open pasture. One steady uphill section. Generally easy underfoot.

Parking: In the National Park car park at Buckden.

Public Transport: Service 71 from Skipton bus station to Buckden (weekends only); Service 800 (Dalesbus) at weekends April-October from Ilkley, Bradford and Leeds.

Refreshment: Buckden – Buck Inn, cafe, shop. The White Lion at Cray and the George at Hubberholme are also on the route. Toilets in Buckden car park.

Maps: OS Outdoor Leisure: Sheet 30 (Yorkshire Dales – Northern and Central); OS Pathfinder SE87/97. Stile Maps: The Dales Way Footpath Map.

BUCKDEN, as its name implies, was once a foresters' settlement and hunting lodge in the royal hunting forest of Langstrothdale. The last village in Upper Wharfedale, it is situated under the flanks of Buckden Pike and makes an excellent starting and finishing point for a walk.

From the car park go through the gate at the top, closing it behind you, and walk along the green track which gradually ascends the hillside – Buckden Rakes. "Rakes" or "raikes" is a northern dialect word for a hill. This particular track is doubly interesting, almost certainly being on the line of Julius Agricola's campaigning road built to subjugate the warlike Celtic Brigante tribes in the first century and originally linking the fort at Ilkley (Olicana) with that at Bainbridge (Virosidium).

It is a well drained limestone track, soon going through a second gate and entering thin, mainly ash, woodland, Rakes Wood. It is a steady climb and you need to take your time, being rewarded by ever more spectacular views across the top of the dale as you ascend.

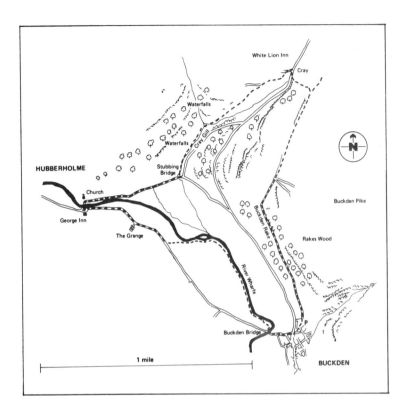

Gradually you emerge from the wood and follow the track as it bears right, through a top gate. The path, less distinct now, levels off and follows the wall through more gates, the path to Buckden Pike soon bearing off right. Keep ahead towards the next gate by a stile but take the path signed to Cray, which leaves by a small pedestrian gate and bears down steep pasture. Take care here as the way is steep as the path bears right towards a wall, to a gate in the bottom corner of the field. Ford the shallow stream (convenient stepping stones can easily be found) to emerge on the road immediately opposite the White Lion Inn at Cray.

The route continues along the farmtrack to the right of the inn, but almost immediately forking to a gate to the right and above the barn ahead, rejoining the farmtrack behind the farm. At the next barn and farm ahead take the narrow, enclosed way between stone walls to the left and below the farm (signed) which leads to a pedestrian gate.

The path is a faint green way which bears slightly right across soft

45

turf above the shoulder of a shallow valley – Cray Gill – before descending.

This is quite a magical place – you are looking into a great green bowl set within the hills that look somehow grander and more spectacular than their height suggests. The intensely green hillside, rocks, scattered trees and tiny beck plunging over a series of a cataracts are like a wild, Romantic painting – a Turner or Caspar Friedrich – made animate.

The way passes the largest of the shimmering waterfalls to a little stone packhorse bridge over Crook Gill, a side valley. Continue alongside the wooded ravine, over an almost hidden bridge of limestone slabs, to reach another stile before you finally join the lane at a gate and stile just west of Stubbing Bridge. Turn right to follow the' lane to Hubberholme.

Hubberholme Church, dedicated to St. Michael and all Angels, dates from Norman times and is a fine example of a small dales church. It was probably a forest chapel in Langstrothdale, as Upper Wharfedale is still known beyond Buckden, and may have occupied a pagan Anglo-Viking burial site. It is built with local stone and roofed with lead from local mines. Its very remoteness probably saved its most remarkable feature, a richly ornamented rood loft, erected in 1558, which survived damage in Civil War times and is one of only two in Yorkshire. The ashes of the Bradford born playwright J.B. Priestley lie scattered in the vicinty – Hubberholme was, understandably, one of his favourite places in the Yorkshire Dales. A plaque in the church recalls his presence.

Also of interest is the George Inn which until relatively recently was owned by the church, being kept by the churchwarden until 1965. It is the scene of the annual "Hubberhome Parliament", a thousand year old tradition during which the vicar auctions the grazing of a 16 acre field, Kirk Pasture, the income so raised being used to help local pensioners.

From the George Inn, walk along the lane towards Buckden for about 400 metres. Go past Grange Farm, to where a gate on the left, a short distance past a barn, gives access to a footpath, part of the Dales Way, which follows a hedge to the riverside. This attractive path follows a long curve of the river embankment over stiles, to join the lane at a field gate. Turn left to Buckden Bridge and walk along the lane up to the village with its ancient green.